The Love Within a Grateful Heart

with Endless Joy and Peace be Plenty

By
Lisa Wake

Grosvenor House
Publishing Limited

All rights reserved
Copyright © Lisa Wake, 2025

The right of Lisa Wake to be identified as the author of this
work has been asserted in accordance with Section 78
of the Copyright, Designs and Patents Act 1988

The book cover is copyright to Lisa Wake

This book is published by
Grosvenor House Publishing Ltd
Link House
140 The Broadway, Tolworth, Surrey, KT6 7HT.
www.grosvenorhousepublishing.co.uk

This book is sold subject to the conditions that it shall not, by way of trade or otherwise, be lent, resold, hired out or otherwise circulated without the author's or publisher's prior consent in any form of binding or cover other than that in which it is published and without a similar condition including this condition being imposed on the subsequent purchaser.

This book is a work of fiction. Any resemblance to
people or events, past or present, is purely coincidental.

A CIP record for this book
is available from the British Library

ISBN 978-1-83615-237-8

The Acknowledgements

With a thankful heart and an endless joy,

I would like to thank everyone for their continued support in my journey, not only in my recovery with my anxiety, but also my journey to reach my goals and dreams with my publishing journey. I am very blessed, I am also very grateful to you all in my experiences, and the chance to help others along the way, my three children, my grandson, my husband, friends past and present and family, to all of you, I love you all lots and very much, I am blessed and grateful to have you all in my life, I am very proud of you all, you are unique, you are special, you are loved.

With special acknowledgements to Alma Farrell and Sue King, two very good, very close friends, both passed from this world, love you both, miss you both xxxx

Dedication

This book of poems is dedicated to all those who are struggling in life and are wanting to find peace, in the little things in life, and to appreciate them, having a better understanding of life and what is given to them, to help learn, grow, endure, embrace, as the unique individuals you all are and the potential you all have to create the positive life you really want, with happiness & dedication you want to give, love be to you all, blessed be to you all.

Live, Laugh, Love Life, you only live once, enjoy it.

About the Author

Lisa is the eldest of six children. She is a mum to three and a nan to one, she lives at the moment in Telford, she has goals and dreams and aspires to reach those goals and dreams. Although her occupation is care & support worker, she has been forced to take time out from work due to crippling anxiety and depression. She has expressed her plans to go back to work. While off work, Lisa has been reflecting, reminiscing, and learning about herself. She still feels there's still some way to go with regards to learning and strengthen herself, but she is growing as she is learning. Lisa finds calm in reading self-help books, listening to her music, and writing both in her journals and writing her poetry. She likes to help others also, and feels her poems that she writes will help in some way, to the best of her abilities, while showing her vulnerability. Lisa hopes you enjoy the creation of her poems as she enjoyed writing them, as you read through her poems that are full of heart and soul with you all in mind.

Contents

Part 1

Chapter one …. Gratitude 1

- Thank you, dear lord.. 3
- Feeling Blessed 4
- Gratefulness is.. 5
- Good morning, good night.. 6
- Your pockets are full 7
- Less is more.. 8
- With a grateful heart 9
- Gratitude...10
- I am 11
- The essence that captures the heart 12
- There's nothing more precious..13
- Dig what you got 14
- When you live 15
- It's a blessing...16
- I have 17
- The greatest gift 18
- How grateful am I 19
- Success is...20
- The stars in my life..21
- Brian 22
- To an old friend 23

Chapter two …. Love 25

- Riley...26
- Finley...27
- Sue...28
- You are very special to me 29
- Spencer 30

Happy valentines	31
When you love someone	32
The love that's never lost	33
Kindness and love	34
A painful goodbye	35
Despite a poem	36
Forever in my heart	37
A song of songs	38
Love has a meaning	40
I know you said	42
The distance between us	43
I miss you	44
The respect you gave me	45
When I look	46
My love for you	47
I never thought I'd miss anyone	48
My love is the light you gave to me	49
Chapter three …. Our imperfections	**51**
I am not perfect	52
I am only human	53
The analogy	54
I may not have a good singing voice	56
Everyone	57
The importance of imperfection	58
We are not perfect	59
Chapter four …. Being yourself	**61**
Unique Me, Unique You	62
May you be	63
Continue	64
You're too nice	65
It's all about you	66
My inner child	67

Peter the potato	68
My cork friends and me	69
My teddy bears and me	70
Why fit in	71
Be you, be true	72
An individual within our shells	73
You don't have to	74
A stitch in time	75
Be true	76
Boundaries	77
Chapter five .... Nature	79
Inspiration and me	80
The love that nature shares	81
The angels of the sky	82
I'm glad I came out	83
Spring is in the air	84
I saw spring today	85
Excuse me Nature	86
Such beauty, such love	87
The tranquil Nature	88
Thank you for visiting me	89
The splendour of Nature	90
How beautiful the Snow	91
I love	92
The rainbow of love and hope	93
Autumn leaves	94
Harmony	95
Bumble bees	96
Good night	97
Nature is	98
In my quiet spot	99
The tree winking	100

When Robins appear	101
How the sea meets the sky	102
Chapter six …. Depression and Anxiety	**103**
The strength you need	104
Never forget how strong you are	105
You are, you can	106
I know I have the strength	107
My mind, an empty room	108
I don't know	110
A dark knight	111
I ventured out	112
Feeling scared	113
Today	114
Believe and go far	115
Hip hip yay	116
Life can be hard	117
When is this trial going to end	118
These are the words	119
I've come so far	120
He's struck again	121
Chapter seven …. Life	**123**
Lives matter, life matters	124
Share the smile	125
You only get one life	126
What is	127
Busy, busy, busy	128
Green, white, and orange	129
Never feel, like you're a burden	130
Sisters in arms	131
For every book	132
Times	133
The injustice of it all	134

Sometimes things don't happen 135
Invisible but real 136
The limits we put on ourselves 137
What life is about 138
Am I here 139
Where do I belong 140
Opportunities and trials 141
Modern technology 142
To connect on such, a deep level 144
I left my heart in Ireland 145
To gain the connection 146
We may have lost you today 147
Life is a risk 148
Why watch the world go by 149
This is not goodbye 150

Part 2 An Introduction to G.D. Bates 153
Scrambled thoughts 155
Forget to remember 156
Moment in time 158
Unconditional 159
Borrowed 160
Shattered reflection 162
Storms of freedom 163
Unwritten reality 164
Where has the festive spirit gone? 166

Part 3 Introduction to Chelsea J Rixon 169
Poppy 171
An endless love for you 172
Through the eyes of the wolf 173
The bully within 174
In the mind 175

A story told	176
Trauma	177
Survivor	178
Through the eyes of a survivor	179
A safe sanctuary for me	180
Unlikely Hero	181
Medication is Hope	182
A gamers life	183

Nowadays people know the price of everything and the value of nothing
– Oscar wilde

The value of life is more precious, and priceless than that of the material things that come in it, I believe that, the material things, are of no value or worth. just a void to fill for a short time of happiness.

Part 1

Chapter one ... Gratitude

With a thankful heart and an endless joy

Thank you, dear Lord

Thank you, dear lord
For seeing me through
To another day
Thank you, dear lord
For the energy, you gave
And sent my way
Thank you, dear lord
For what, I was able, to do
Thank you, dear lord
For getting, me through
Today I was able
To do, more than I thought
With the strength
That I, had sought
Grateful am I, for what you did
I thank you, dear lord
For the opportunities
You do give
Thank you, dear lord
And heavenly father too
Thank you both
For being you

22nd March 2024

Feeling Blessed

Feeling blessed
Waking to, a new day
Shining through the curtains
To create a smile, that just won't fade

Feeling blessed
I have, all my limbs intact
All my senses. Are working hard
And my organs, are quick to act

Feeling blessed
A roof, over my head
With clothes, on my back
And a place to rest, calling it a bed

Feeling blessed
My children, and grandchildren too
All my friends, and all my family
In this world, so very cool

I am blessed
I am grateful
I am loved
I am stable

16th February 2024

Gratefulness is

Gratefulness is a gift
It gives you joy and peace
Gratefulness is a blessing
Of the small gifts, that we receive
Gratefulness is a sign
Of love, and of hope
Gratefulness is a smile
Giving tranquillity and calm
Gratefulness is a treasure
That costs, nothing at all
Gratefulness is the people we see
All our loved ones, we hold dear
Close, to me and thee

13th January 2024

Good morning, good night

Good morning and good night
I do say to you all
My darlings, incredible and bright
To your pictures
I look at, everyday
Thomas, Amy, Patrick and Paul
And to Finley, my sweet darling babe
Harmony and also Lotti
My, how I love you all
Good morning, good night
To you Chuck Norris
Good morning, good night
My love, my solace
Good morning, good night
I am truly blessed
Good morning, good night
I am grateful, you're all the best

Started 3rd April 2024
Finished 10th April 2024

Your Pockets are Full

You don't get what you want
Only what you need
Your pockets are full
When you have everything
Roof over your head
Food in your belly
When you have friends
And your family
Children and grandchildren
Your mum and dad too
Brothers, and sisters
Aunts, uncles, cousins
Nieces and nephews too
Your pockets are full
If, you have all
No need to murmur
No need to moan
About life's luxuries
That you don't have
You don't get, what you want in life
Only what, you need
Your pockets are full
When you have everything

18th April 2023

Less is more

They say less is more
That, I can say, is very true
After years, of buying and hoarding
I finally made, that breakthrough
Years of clutter, I need to rehome
Is being sorted, out to go
So much happier, I feel now
And much lighter, there's no doubt
Less is more, a smile on my face
Grinning, from ear to ear
I may not have very much
But I have everything
I hold dear

19th April 2023

With a Grateful Heart

With a grateful heart
I am here today
With a grateful heart
A smile, that is here, to say
With a grateful heart
I know, tomorrow, will come
With a grateful heart
I am safe, in a home
With a grateful heart
I have everyone I need
With a grateful heart
Everything too, indeed
Upon the hearth of my heart
A warm glow ascends
With, a welcome, that does not part
And a smile, that never ends
Thank you, from the, very start
With my very, grateful heart

31st July 2023

Gratitude

Tis the little things
That's left with gratitude
Makes the biggest blessings

Tis the tiniest things
Felt with love
Giving the world, it's dressings

Tis the gratefulness
That you have
The happier you will feel

Tis being happy
For everyone you have
Will make your life, easier to heal

Tis true gratitude
And a dose of hope
To make life, so much greater

Tis a pleasure
A bonus, not leisure
To have such a gift
A life, to treasure

Tis in life
You get what you need
Helping you through
Your life indeed
Be thankful, be grateful
And happy too
With, the gifts given
And honour, them through

18th June 2023

I Am

I am grateful
To see the sun rise, each morning
And the stars, twinkle at night

I am grateful
To hear, the raindrops falling
And a baby laughing, in daylight

I am grateful
To feel the snow, so cold
And the flowers of spring, so bright

I am grateful
To touch, the life, I have
And what it holds, for me after tonight

I am grateful
To love my children, grandchildren too
And my teddy bears, are all in sight

I am grateful
To taste opportunities, that come my way
And the food, that's a delight

I am grateful
To laugh at jokes, told by you
That sense of humour, is what I like

The seven wonders of the world
Gifts we hold so dear
To see, to feel, to touch, to taste
To love, to laugh, to hear

6th July 2023

The essence that captures the heart

Sitting in nature
With it's calming embrace
Opens, my heart wide
And teaches my soul, to fly
The influence, that calming essence
The gentile nature, does give
It captures the heart
The mind, and the soul
Thus, to motivate, us to live
It excites me, to come out here
To come, and sit with you
The amazing grace
You do be giving
Sweetness, is the sound
Of the angels, living
That fly, all around
Enlightens me
And guides, me too
The essence, of nature
That calms me, through and through

27th March 2024

There's nothing more precious

There's nothing more precious, than family
I am grateful for mine
There's nothing more precious
Then your children, and grandchildren too
My love for them, is divine
There's nothing more precious
Then the love, you share
With those, that surround you
To show, that you care
There's nothing more precious
Then the moments, you get
To hear the laughter
And the joys, I'm truly blessed
These are more precious
Even more so, than gold
There's nothing more precious
Then your family
Love them, and cherish them, and keep hold

18th April 2024

Dig what you got

Dig what you got now
Because you're not
Going to have it forever
Dig what you got now
Don't blow it
Not now, not ever
Appreciate your life
And who you have in it
Be grateful, for your life
And what, you have in it
Because you never know
One day, you could lose it all

Started 10th April 2024
Finished 11th April 2024

    Inspired by an episode of Happy Days, season 2, episode 10 called "A star is bored" where Fonzie (Henry Winkler) says "dig what you got"

When you live

When you live, and love
With all your heart
One life, is all you need

When you live, and love
From, the very start
The treasure, you will give indeed

To live, and love
With all your heart
The gift, that keeps giving

To live, and love
From, the very start
Enables, you positive living

A heart full of love
A soul, full of joy
And a life, worth enduring

Started 11th Apil 2024
Finished 12th April 2024

                        Inspired by the 2024 film called "10 live"

It's a Blessing

Every morning, that I wake
It's a blessing
Every moment that I smile
It's a blessing
Every second, my heart beats
It's a blessing
Every day the sun shines, and the birds fly
It's a blessing
Every time I look at my children, my grandson too
It's a blessing
Every mealtime I am fed and watered through
It's a blessing
Every week I have clothes on my back
It's a blessing
Every month I have a roof over my head
It's a blessing
For every breath that I do take
It's a blessing
And every word I did Spake
It's a blessing
To have my organs, my limbs, and my senses intact
It's a blessing
To have the support, when I need it the most
It's a blessing
To be able to live, to love, to laugh, and to hope
It's a blessing
Today the sun shined
Today, I smiled
Today, I am fully blessed
Today, I am grateful, for the very best
It's a blessing, beyond belief
It's a blessing, with relief
You may not be able, to count all your blessings
As, there are so many
But to name your blessings, one by one
Take care, and be ready

1st June 2024

I have

I have my music
I have my books
I have pens and paper
I'm happy, come take a look

I have a roof, over my head
I have food, in my belly
I have clothes on my back
Who needs a telly

My organs work
My limbs do too
My senses work also
Why should I feel blue

I have my children
Also, my grandson
Riley, my kitten
And my husband, eating a bun

I have my family, and my friends
And each day I wake to
I have each breath that I take
And each step to get through

What more do I need
When I have what I have
Nothing is the answer
For I am grateful, for my life

5th December 2024
Completed 6th December 2024

The Greatest Gift

The greatest gift
Is the love we share
The gift that we were blessed with
That we may care

The greatest gift
We were given
To love one another
No judgements nor friction

The greatest gift
That we did gain
A blessing to all
There's no shame, don't refrain

The greatest gift
Our brother too, did bare
Was given, by our father, in heaven
And natures love, we now declare

7th December 2024

How grateful am I

Bright as a daisy
Bright as a sunflower
Bright as the sun
Shining, with all its power
To light up the day
Cheering us on
Helping us, on our way
At the break of dawn

Happy is the sunshine
Happy is nature
Happy are the people
And the creator
To welcome, every colour
Every shape and size too
How grateful am I
For everything, pure and true

Completed 29th November 2023

Success is

Waking up in the morning
With a smile
Getting up in the morning
To walk another mile
Feeling your heart beating
Keeping you alive
Putting food in your belly
Ensure you survive
Loving others from deep within
The love you want to share
And to let, your loved ones know
That you really care
Seeing the day, right through to night
No matter how good, or bad
Pursuing your goals and dreams
Helping you, to feel glad
It's not the money, you got in your pocket
Whether it's cash or card
Nor the material things in life
That blows your world apart
It's the simple things in life
That really shows what success is
To live, love, and laugh
You can't deny it's this
This is, what success is

Started 5th January 2025
Finished 6th January 2025

The Stars in my Life

The lights glisten in my eyes
Like stars, the night skies
The lights in mine eyes
Are the lights of my life
The lights, I am grateful for
That shine so bright
Those stars, are my children
One, two, and three
My beautiful grandson
And my kitten Riley
They are all incredible
And they are amazing
The twinkling in mine eyes
Are the stars in my life
Perfect, cherished, and loving

Started 2nd January 2025
Finished 16th January 2025

Brian

We may not have, a lot in common
But one thing, that we do
Three incredible children
And a grandson, we both love, true
We were together once
I wasn't able to satisfy
My struggles with anxiety and depression
I just, couldn't comply
Mistakes made on both sides
Along with parts to play too
Boundaries, I could not set
And just wanted to please
Working together, better now
The friendship, we now have
For a better understanding
Of each other's needs
To help our children
Our grandson too
To ease their burdens
To help them, and each other through
I am grateful, to have a friend in you

24th September 2023

To an old Friend

I spoke to an old friend, the other night
The spark was shining, oh so very bright
Made the night, seem like daylight

The chat was relaxed, and fully authentic
Honest, fun and energetic
Yet seriously magnetic

A smile and a laugh, that was shared
Between two friends, who really cares
True vulnerability also, was bared

To an old friend, how special you are
The comfort you give, from your heart
Non-judgemental, a blessing, from the start

To an old friend, a soul full of joy
To an old friend, a blessing to employ
To an old friend, your friendship, I do enjoy

        Thank you to an amazing friend, you're a dream and a
            delight that will never end. Thank you xxx

Started 15th January 2024
Finished 27th January 2024

Chapter two

Love

Shines a light

Riley

Riley, my kitten new
My tuxedo kitten, black and white
With a goatee too
He wiggles his bum
Ready to pounce
Zooming around the home
Without a second glance
He bats his paper balls
Right back at me
He looks out the window to see, what he can see
With his meows, to go out
Or to come in
Riley waits patiently
At the door, bless him
Riley knows the times
Of the meals, that he has
He's the alarm clock
When time comes to pass
Riley, Riley
My wee bonnie lad
With a fun and loving character
A beautiful boy, he's not bad

7th December 2024

Finley

A fine young man born, into this world
In his mum's arms, loved so very much
Never a dull moment, with this happy boy
Laughing and playing, with fun and joy
Every moment, is special and pure
Yet, also precious and secure

Loving, so much, your cheeky smile
On and on, it glows
Very lifting and complete
Every time, your smile flows

Never feel, you're on your own
Always here, to hold you close
No matter how far the distance
My love for you, always glistens

I love you very much, my sweet little darling
Love from nan xxx

21st February 2023

Sue

In memory of a lady, so kind and sweet
Her love and warmth, a treasure to keep
Her smile could lighten, up the darkest night
Her laughter, a melody, so pure and bright
Though she's gone, her spirit will live on
In the memories of those, she shone upon
Her kindness and love, a legacy so grand
Forever cherished, in the hearts, of the land
In every act of kindness, we'll see your face
A reminder of your beauty, and your grace
You'll remain our friend, even with your wings
Our hearts full, when you sing
But we will look, for your star in the sky
And to know, that this is never, a goodbye

Written by Chelsea J Rixon

A dedication to sue, who passed 15th July 2024
Cherished by all who loved her so xxxx

You are very special to me

You are all, very special, to me
Thomas, Amy, Patrick, and Finley
You are all, very special to me
Very proud am I, to be
A mum and a nan, just to you
To love, and to cherish, to see you through
The unconditional love, that I have for you all
Is unwavering, it won't fall through
You are all, very special, to me
Here's my hand, I will be here
Being there to give you the hand
To you all so dear
To help you all, to the best I can
My hopes for you all, are so very high
Your dreams ready, to come alive
You are all, so very special, to me
Thus, I hope, that you can see

I am very proud of you all
I love you all dearly xxxx

6th June 2024

Spencer

There is a beautiful dog
His name in Spencer
He plays, and has fun
With a family, which he did enter

There is a beautiful dog
His love knows no bounds
He loves to go on his walks
Sharing his love around

There is a beautiful dog
With brown socks on his paws
A big black cuddly fur baby
Protecting you and yours

There is a beautiful dog
Greets you at the door
Happy to see you
Smiling, all the more

There is a beautiful dog
He is now at rest
His love will be missed
But Spencer, is the best

There is a beautiful dog
Oh, what a joy he has been
A blessing to have known you boy
In our hearts you will, forever be

2nd June 2024

Happy Valentines

The day I married you
And you, married me
Two hearts beat, endlessly
Doors, were opened
To a new life, for us
A life of potential
A gift, and a blessing, from above

Fourteen years later
We are still, you and me
When God made you
He knew, what you'd need
Someone daft, crazy, cheeky, and bonkers
Crackers and fun loving too
So, that very woman, he sent, your way
Was ……. guess who

Started 14th February 2024
Finished 15th February 2024

When you love someone

They say, if you love someone
You have to let them go
I have tried that, already
It didn't work, my feelings grow
I think about him, every day
every night too
So, this is what, I'm going to say
Telling it to you
When you love someone
Really love someone
It's a feeling, you cannot ignore
Go in search, for them
Travel across, the shore
But what if, they can't remember me
Don't want to know me
Or, with somebody else already
The only way, to find that out
Is to go find them
Give them, a shout
That's the only, way to know
Don't let your fear
Stop you in your tracks
With threats, of the unknown
Instead, take a breath, get up and go
You are not alone
When you carry
Their heart, next to yours
Have a picture of them, in your mind
They are locked, so deep
Within your soul
And the memories, that you carry
That you, once shared
Are never, left behind
When you love someone
Really love, them true
Taken the opportunities
To go find them
And see, it through

26th March 2024

The Love that's never lost

When you love someone
So very dear
It's never lost
And it never disappears
To love someone
You hold dear
They may seem, so far apart
Yet they are near
In your heart
And in your soul
You don't have
Very far to go
Just close your eyes
They, will be
Stood in front, of you
So that, you may see
With a smile
To comfort you
And the love
To see you through
Letting you know
They are safe
And their love, is close by
That there is, definitely
Not a goodbye

14th March 2024

Kindness & Love

Kindness and love
Is what we need the most
Kindness and love
Are my favourite hosts
Kindness and love
Is for life, not just for Christmas
Kindness and love
With smiles, hugs, and kisses

Kindness and love
To show that we care
Kindness and love
To say we are there
Kindness and love
With tears and laughter
Kindness and love
Forever more and after

16th January 2025

A Painful Goodbye

I see a white feather, upon the ground
Tis you, I am thinking of
I pick it up, the feather so white
Tis you I feel, your arms, around

I can't expect you, to wait for me
Tis not fair, on you, I see
Although, that is what, I do right now
Waiting for you, somewhere, somehow

I love you now, I love you forever
That, I can be sure
But to let you go, I must do
This pain, I will endure

I miss you, but never forget you
The sickening feeling, inside
As I miss, your banter and craic
From you, I will not hide

8th June 2023

Despite a Poem

Despite a poem, I wrote three months ago
I cannot, forget you
Despite a poem, I wrote three months ago
I cannot, stop thinking about you
Your smile I see, in my mind
Lights up my heart
My soul wants to find
The delicate kiss
That just doesn't, want to miss
A tender touch
Giving so much
An incredible cuddle
We're nestled close, in a huddle
Your Amazing smiles
Lighting the paths, for miles
The stars in your eyes
As I look deep
Makes my heart
Go skip, skip, beat
And my smile, lights the room
Like a Christmas tree
As thoughts of you, are right up close to me
Despite a poem, I wrote three months ago
I love you, love you so

14th September 2023

Forever in my Heart

Forever in my heart
You will be
Forever in my heart
You will stay
Locked up, right in here
Never, ever to fade away
My love for you
Is forever, so strong
Sometimes, I am unsure
If, I can carry on
With the love, I have for you
Goes, with the respect
That is there for you too
Grateful my heart
Grateful my soul
Genuine the man
Friendship, forever, I will hold
Forever in my heart
A picture I carry
Forever in my heart
A memory, that is happy

23rd October 2023

A Song of Songs

On this day I will be here
Spending my time
Wherever you are near
This I promise you
Never to leave your side
And all the love, in the world
Until the time is through
Now and forever, to you I belong
From this moment, Tamry
You are the one
The king of my heart
Nothings gonna change my love for you
It's you I wanna grow old with
And never to be apart
Bringing out the best in me
There you are, there you'll be
I knew I loved you
Not a day goes by
I'm crazy for you, I need you now
No matter what
My forever love, is right here waiting
And even though, I haven't met you yet
You'll be in my heart
I'll be loving you forever, no regrets
I miss you like crazy
Love really hurts without you
Your love is all that I need
I just can't stop loving you
I can't even sleep
Baby can I hold you, every day I love you
When will I see you again
So, to cherish every moment too
With my life, in your arms
But if I let you go
The sacred trust, that I have
Like the lighthouse, shining bright

Suddenly, missing you
Will burn and cut deep inside
With the hurt and the pain, like no other
There be, no place, I can hide

20th November 2023

    A compilation of song titles from many songs combined together,
        to create a heartfelt meaningful creation into a poem

Love Has a Meaning

I want to, make you feel
So incredibly real
I'd like to make you feel
Loved, wanted, happy and content
I'd love to make you feel
Cherished, adored, warm, free with respect
You're the reason, I wake every morning
And the reason, I believe in love
A picture in my heart, a memory in my soul
Love has a meaning
With you I can't let go
My heart, feels full
My soul, so whole
Cuddled up, right next to you
My feelings carry me away
You make my heart feel
Like it's summer every day
When I want to feel, you close to me
My heart jumps, as I close my eyes
And skips, a few beats
Here I am I love with you
Achieving something
No-one else could do
You're bringing out the best in me
The man I adore, who giving all
More than eyes, could ever see
And more than words, could ever say
The special nurturer
I hope to meet, one day
My light, my strength
Your nurturing speciality
Grows at length, very happily
You are someone very real
Very special too
With your smile, the real deal
I surrender my heart, to you

Denying the love, that I have
To you that would not be true
But to hold, to grow, and have a laugh
I know I'm home, with you

21st November 2023

I know you said

I know you said
You couldn't expect me to wait, for you
But I have been
And I still do

You are the one
Who showed me this level
The love, I now know exists
From you, the one, who is special

You showed me respect
Even encouraged me too
You gave me everything, asked for nothing
Your banter and craic, stopped me feeling blue
You are the one
I am blessed, to have known
The gentle man, I miss like crazy
My love for you has so grown

You're the reason
I wake, and get up each morning
The reason I smile
As the day, is dawning

You are the last thing
And the first thing, on my mind
As I settle, down at night
The morning breaks, and I find
The tears I shed, warmth I feel
With my eyes closed, I see you, heart and mind
It makes, this feeling, incredibly real
There's no way, I can leave, you behind

I know you said
You couldn't, expect me, to wait for you
My heart and soul, is whole and full
I will wait forever, and forever wait for you

17th December 2023

The distance between us

It's the physical distance
Keeping us apart
The closest we are
Is through our heart
In my soul
Is where you reside
Within my mind
Keeping you alive
With memories and cuddles
I'd like to share
And into each other's eyes
We do both stare
With a smile or two
Our hearts, won't feel blue
Your heart of gold
You won't be left
Out in the cold
You're the diamond
That shines bright
On an island, beautiful and light
With so much craic
And so much fun
The humour you have
Just won't, be glum
The distance between us
Is only physical
But my love for you
Is forever and unconditional

29th December 2023

I Miss You

I miss you, so very much
While in my thoughts
I feel your tender touch
To close my eyes
There you are, in front of me
In my dreams
I'm in your company
My heart so full
My soul is too
When my thoughts
They are of you
The songs, they play
In my head, and out loud
Tears, they fall, as the lyrics
Show my feelings, for you, up in the cloud
I wish I could be with you
To comfort you now
Being there with you
Helping you out somehow
I miss you everyday
Every week, every month, every year
This I have to say
I love you, and I miss you my dear

17th January 2025

The respect you gave me

I love you Tam
My very beautiful, special man
I adore you, want to hug you Cuddle you, and help you
My heart beats, with excitement
While my thoughts, are of you
You showed me, what love really is
Pulled me up to a level, I never knew exists
You're in my soul
Where I feel whole
You're my hearts inspiration
to helping with, my motivation
I love you, more than words, can say
This, will never, fade away
The conversations, we once had
Made me feel, so very glad
I still remember, conversations, a few
Love to have, you here, for a brew
You respected me, encouraged me
Uplifted me, laughed with me
And above all, helped me
To chase my dreams, hold them tight
Though you're not here
In my heart, and my soul
You are very near
You are very, special to me
In this, I feel my love for thee
Deeply, and free
Though my feelings, aren't in my words
They are however, in my heart
Flying freely, just like the birds
In my soul, and in my heart
Hoping, one day, they can be heard

Started 5th January 2024
Finished 13th January 2024

When I look

When I look, at a picture of you
I say, hello my love
How do you do
Hope you had, a good night sleep
Have a good day today
And my heart, takes a leap
My imagination, starts running wild
Thinking of you,
And your amazing smile
I wriggle into, the back of my chair
As I imagine, you are here
Cuddling and comforting, me right there
With plenty of love, to share my dear
When I look, at a picture of you
I say, hello sweetheart
Hope you had, a good day through
Have a good night
Hope to see you soon

12th March 2024

My Love for you

My love for you
Is more than a feeling
More than an emotion
More than, a want, or a needing

My love for you
Is stronger than a tornado
Deeper than the ocean
Hotter than a volcano

It's the reaching out
And the tender touch
A precious moment
Two hearts beating together, much

It's in our eyes
We're yet to lock
And our lips
That we may talk

It's in the memories, to be made
In joy, and in sorrow
It's two souls, becoming one
In sync with each other,
in a future tomorrow
It's in the help, I want to give
To strengthen you
It's in my smile, to show
My love for you

Started 18th April 2024
Finished 26th April 2024

I never thought, I'd miss anyone

I never thought, I'd miss anyone
As much as, I miss you
But as per, your request
When I said, I love you
To concentrate on my marriage, I am in
As hard as it is, to do
Five years on, is the same today
My feelings for you
Have not, gone away
Your amazing smile
And the chats, we had
The way, you went, that extra mile
Made me feel glad
That I knew you
If only, to talk too
We never, met in person
But my feelings, are stronger
I never thought, I'd miss anyone
As much as I miss you
In the past, and the present
Also, the future, too
I shall wait, forever
Cause I'm, so in love with you

16th March 2024

My love is the light you gave to me

My busy bee
The king of my heart
My love for you
Is forever here, never to part
My love for you is the light
That be shining through
In the darkest night
The rip in the curtain
The beam is shining bright
Shining full with love
Giving beautiful light
Home to a dove
The littlest bee
Which I carry with me
Has me feeling safe and happy
The strength inside
That which I have
With my thoughts of you
Is my heart and soul combined
Beating so fast, skipping beats
And being so, very full
100% through, no it's not dulled
I love you, miss you
I adore you, very much too
I yearn for you, pine for you
I long for your hugs, pure and true
Your arms wrapped around me
Keeping me safe and warm
I will wait forever
And forever wait for thee

16th March 2025

Chapter three
Our Imperfections
Are our perfections

I am not Perfect

I am not perfect
You will see
But please, please
Don't dis me
I was created
By just one man
Before, I came to earth
To be, who I am
I am not perfect
And don't claim, to be
I say the wrong things
Make mistakes, you may see
Yes, I pay the price
For they, aren't free
I am not perfect
But, I have emotions
And feelings, of plenty
I am not perfect
But neither, am I empty
However, I am only human
Who has, her flaws
Included, in her personality
I am not perfect
As well, you know
My character, and personality
Will help me, to grow
Like all humans
I get frustrated, and want to scream
I am not perfect
As I'd like, to be
But I can dream

24th March 2024

I am only Human

I am human, very real
And make mistakes, I do
I may say, the wrong things
Letting others down
But perfect, I am not
I'd be lying, if I said I am

I am, only human
With feelings and emotions
Also, very real and true
And the conscience, with them, too
I have, so much love, in me
That which, I want to give
But struggle, to love, just one man
At a time, how, do I live

I am only human
With guilt, getting, the better of me
Going to bed, I cry myself, to sleep
Perhaps, I should be, on my own
No-one would get hurt, or get, let down
Do I care? Yes, I do
I am human, after all, very real
Right the way, through

1st February 2024

The Analogy

Imagine a thorn
Are the mistakes, we make in life
And the bed we lay in
Is the life, we lead, in daylight
As we turn over
In our beds at night
We catch and lean
On a thorn, in the right side
Pointy and sharp
Is the torn, where we lay
Ouch, we yelp
I need help, today
I can't believe that I moved, right there
I'll be watching
When I move, should I dare
I won't be making
That same mistake
I will lie elsewhere
Just give me a break
Each night, I learn
Where not to move
So, to wake up
With the groove
Refreshed and, without pain
Smiles and joy, even in the rain
As I stretch, counting, one, two and three
I am learning, now can you see?
This is how we can learn
Not to make, the same, mistake twice
Now we can go, and grow
Move on and endure
While embracing our lives
And mistakes, for sure
We make mistakes

That's what we do
We are, only human
We will learn, and possibly get through
Maybe, very soon

                    Inspired by a dream I had, using the very same analogy
                              as was used in my dream

Started 17th October 2023
Finished 24th October 2023

I may not have a good singing voice

I may not have, a good singing voice
I know, I can sing out of tune
Nevertheless, I have a voice
Just the same as you
I can talk, I can laugh
Even shout out loud
I may not have, a good singing voice
Instead, I'll hum to the clouds
This special gift, we have been given
In this, you may agree
To have noise, come out our mouths
Very blessed are we
I may not have, a good singing voice
But understanding, is needed, you see
There are poor souls, in this world
Who cannot, make a sound, to them blessed be
It does not make them less important
Or us any more
We all live in, this same world
No matter, how near, or far
There is gratitude,
In what, we can do
No matter, how different, we are
Coming together, to help, one another through
To help, those in need, go far

14th October 2023

Everyone

Everyone, has baggage
Everyone, has a past
No-one is perfect
Even down, to the last
Everyone, makes mistakes
Myself included too
We tend, to take, the wrong turn
Decisions, we regret, soon
No-one is exempt
From the choices, we make in life
So long as we can learn, from them
In this we can survive
Everyone has a dark side
Also, a light side too
What you choose to show in life
Is entirely, up to you
I choose, to show, my light side
Though my dark side, creeps in
Leaving me, with guilt
Which cuts, very deep within
Yes, this makes us human
And human, we all be
It doesn't mean, we can't get on
We're all the same, you see
I have made my mistakes
I'm sure, you have too
Let us join together
And help each through

2nd April 2023

The Importance of Imperfection

No-one is exempt
From imperfection
Not me, not you
Nor the boys, or girls, in blue
The perfection we have, as humans
Is the imperfection, we actually are
Naturally imperfect
To carry us wide and far
Helping us to learn, and grow
The perfect life, we are in
To be imperfect, maybe a blow
It's what makes us, individuals within
One thing, is for sure
Our imperfection, is so pure
To be perfectly, imperfect
We should embrace
To open the doors
And use the space

24th August 2023

We are not perfect

I say, we're not perfect
In theory, we are
Our imperfections, are perfect
They are our guiding stars
The imperfections, are what makes us
Our characters, by far
Flaws and weaknesses
Disabilities, as well
The vulnerabilities, that we have
Shall we show, and tell
They say, we're not perfect
Guess what, that's not true
Our imperfections, are our teachers
Helping us, to get through
If we didn't have, imperfections
We would learn nothing
But, we have to make mistakes
In order to learn something
I am not perfect
And, don't plan to be
However, I do plan
To be, and to do
To the best, of my abilities
To be perfect, would be boring
But, that would be, a different story

Started 28th March 2024
Finished 29th March 2024

Chapter four

Being yourself

Being true, right through

Unique Me, Unique You

This is me, I am one
There is only one as unique as me
Uniquely individual, you can see
My disabilities, my strengths, my weaknesses too
Makes me unique, in my individual way, cool
My flaws, my experience, my mistakes, my character
My religion, my life, my colour, my fun-factor
This is what, makes me, me
The one and only, unique individual me

This is you, you are one
There is only one as unique as you
Uniquely individual, I can see
Your disabilities, your strengths, your weaknesses too
Makes you unique, in your individual way, cool
Your flaws, your experience, your mistakes, your character
Makes you completely different, even your fun-factor
This is what makes you, you
The one and only, individual unique you

Everyone is different, in their individual ways
Everyone is special, in their own unique way
Unique me, unique you
Unique individuals, through and through

April 2018

May you be

May you be happy
May you be healthy
May you be safe and warm
To be living, in peace
And in harmony
Feeling, very strong

May you be loved
May you be comforted
May you be, secure
To live with laughter
And with hope
With a life, to help, you endure

May you have wisdom
May you embrace
May your gratefulness
Always leave a trace
And your knowledge too
Shared with grace

Be happy
Be healthy
Be safe and warm
Living in peace, sheltered from the storm

3rd January 2024

Continue

Continue to grow
Continue to shine
Nothing is perfect
All of the time
This is what, I shall do
Continue, as I started
And follow, right through
I have come, so very far
Even started, to raise, my own bar
I'm starting to learn
A bit about, myself
With self-reflection
Self-care, and self-love
Still, I have, a way to go
With that bar, in my life
It's there, to help me grow
Every time, I raise that bar
I'm pushing myself, to excel
So, I will, continue, to go far

Started 24th March 2024
Finished 25th March 2024

You're too nice

You're too nice
Is what you say
But I can't be
Any other way
This is, who I am
This is me
Yes, I give a damn
Kind and loving
Full of heart
Grateful and positive
Loyal and trusting, from the start
I am, the one and only
Just as you are too
A uniquely created, individual
Right the way through
I am, what I am
A human, with a heart
I am, who I am
Someone, who cares
Wholey, from the start
You're too nice
That is what, you say
Perhaps, I'll save that chat
For another day

24th March 2024

It's all about you

You can only find yourself
When you find a way
To love yourself
Take some time out
Reflect on you
Self-care, and self-love
Is what you're gonna do
It doesn't matter
Who others, think you are
What you say
Or what, you can do, by far
Matter it does, though
Who you, think you are
You can be anything
Even, a bright, shining star
Just take time out
Focus on you
Treat yourself
For, it's all about you

12th March 2024

My Inner child

My inner child
Is starting, to break out
Beware, my dear, beware
The fun loving, and free spirit
Is coming out
Only stop her, if you dare
Let her be, let her play
She is happy, and full of joy
The positive nature
Of my inner child, so content
Has the ability, to employ
Fun and games
Laughter and peace
Comfort and love, so true
Why not, join in, with her
And embrace it all, too

19th February 2024

Peter the Potato

I had a friend
Come to visit, before Christmas
Came, with his family and friends
Still, he is here, today
More than likely, to his end
Sat in his chair, upon the side
Watching us, as we, come and go
Ageing, very gracefully, he is
His name, is Peter the potato
With a smile, upon his face
Scarf on his body, muffs on his ears too
Keeping warm, dry, and safe
Thank goodness, he does not, need the loo

19th February 2024

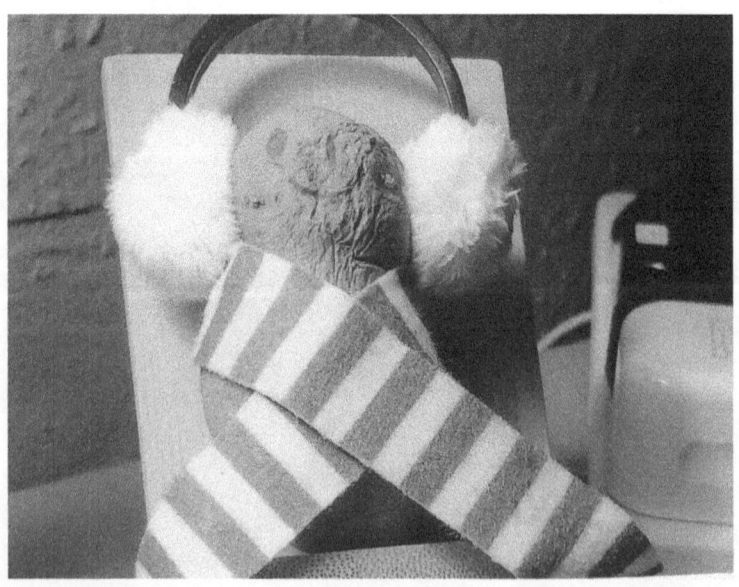

My Cork friends and me

I have three friends in cork
Smiles on their faces, they do have
Unfortunately, they cannot talk
But in a row, they do stand
Very friendly, but very small
Tiny, you would say
Standing at under, two inches tall
Greeting whoever, comes through the door
With the smiles, of joy for you to adore
To uplift you, and spread glee
That would be
My three cork friends, and me

Started 15th February 2024
Finished 16th February 2024

My Teddy Bears and me

I kiss, my teddy bears
Good morning and good night
I talk to my teddies, each day
To ask, if they're alright
I keep them warm
With the blankets, I made
Cuddling up to them
Loving them my way
A wink here, a smile there
For each, and every teddy bear
To comfort my cuddly, loyal friends
It may be hard to comprehend
But for me, it's very simple
I love my bears, cuddly and little
Their little smiles, upon their faces
Fills me with joy, and with graces
My teddy bears and me
Inner child too, you'll see
Gathered together, to go hand in hand
Come together, to form our own band
To love and comfort, one another
Me and my teddy bears
Together always, and forever

21st July 2023

Why Fit in

Why fit in
When you were born, to stand out
An individual, that you are
The person, you are, about
There is no shame
To whom you are
Nor a crime to shine your light
A beautiful people
You all, are to me
Individuals, in your, own right
Tis good to be different
Tis good to be you
You don't need to fit in
Invest in yourself, be true
Care for yourself
Love who you are
The potential, I know you have
Is a gift, that will take you far
Believe in you,
And what you can do
Don't give up,
You can see this through
Just remember the person, you are
The place where you have been
And the distance, you have come far
Share your love
Share your peace
Share your individuality too

18th December 2023

Be you, Be true

Staying true to yourself, and to others
Authentically, being very real
We may not come, with certificates
But in this, we can feel
It does not matter, what others think
Or what they say, or do
Now is the time, to do your, own thing
And just believe, in you
Turn your cant's into cans
And your dreams, into plans
In this, you will, get through
Blessed be your energy
That you bring, to the table
Your gratefulness, for what, you have
Tis this, that makes you able
Your own individuality
Is of most importance
And by far, what counts
Your own unique, and special ways
Tis this, that will mount
And guide you, through your days
Be you, be true
You will never, be feeling blue

28th January 2024

An individual within our shells

There is, within our shells
An individual, that you seek
Here is me, just one individual
Do you fancy, taking a peek
I have my flaws, my weaknesses too
That I can confirm
Strengths and talents, I also have
They all stand, quite firm

There is, within my shell
An individual, in my own right
I have everything, that makes me, who I am
No approval needed, this is me, alright
My methods of dealing, with different situations
May not be approved, or ethical, of others
But the method to my madness, to solve problems
Has worked well, through the years

There is, within my shell
An individual, full of heart
Feelings and emotions, that I have
No judgments, and kind, from the start
Just remember, who you are
Where you have been
You've come so far
Embrace your own individuality
Let you and your smile, be seen

10th December 2023

You don't have to

You don't have to impress other people
To get what you want in life
You don't have to, please other people
To get where you want in life
You don't have to be other people
To be who, you want to be in life
You don't have to supress yourself
To be satisfied in life
Be you, be happy
Be free, be dappy
Embrace you, and your, individuality
Embrace your inner child
And your personality
Embrace the freedom, trying to get out
Life is like a rollercoaster, throwing you about
We get one chance, in this world
Be grateful, be free
Have fun, you'll see

2nd October 2023

A Stitch in Time

A stitch in time
Tis not a crime
It's all the rage, and all the fun
With laughing, is never done
It's the laughter, shared with others
Contagious, as it may well be
With sisters and brothers
Family, friends and strangers, blessed be
So, turn those frowns upside down
And give your laughs, for free
North, south, east, and west
All round the world, will see
A stitch in time, through the laughter
Tis the best life, indeed

27th August 2023

Be True

Being true to yourself
Can be, extremely hard
The truths, you will find
In whom you are
But to be true
Tis the best thing, to do
Self-reflection, through self-care
Brings about the hero,
Deep down in there
Be not ashamed, of who you are
Or what you do, you will go far
Just remember, these few words
Unique you are, unique you be
Be true to yourself,
You will be free
In this you will see

17th July 2023

Boundaries

Be not afraid
To create your boundaries
But please stand firm
Once you do
The boundaries, you have formed
Are long overdue
But better you will feel
Through and through
The creation of your boundaries
To others, they will confirm
That you, are no, walk over
And this they, will learn
They may pile, the pressure on
To make you crumble, and weak
But reach, for the hero, deep inside
And know, you are, strong and unique

6th July 2023

Chapter five

Nature

At it's very best

Inspiration and me

A snowball of inspiration
Coming my way
Lots of ideas, for the poems
I write, each day
Be it in nature
In my quiet spot
Around the corner
Whether it be, cold or hot
Or be it, in my home
Where peace and tranquillity
Wants to roam
When I am, on my own
I close my eyes
A deep breath, I take
The stillness, comes alive
I take a break
Letting inspirations glow
Shining brighter, to me
I'm happy to follow
And work, with inspiration
Working as a team
Inspiration and me

Started 24th March 2024
Finished 25th March 2024

The love that nature shares

The love, that nature shares
Goes to show, how much, she cares
Humble and bright
A colourful, and precious, delight
With her warmth and comforting ways
Gives uplifting, in top form
With her cheerful, and charmful, rays
Providing healing, to you
With tranquil and calm
Trying to keep you
Safe from harm
Helping you, to smile
Inside and out
Going the extra mile
Trusting and sacrificing herself
Selflessly, to you, without a doubt
This is the love that nature shares
Showing how much, she really cares

18th March 2024

The Angels of the sky

My, how they fly
The angels, of the sky
They fly low
They fly high
Spreading their wings
To soar, right on by
My, how they sing
The angels, with the sounds, they bring
Hello up there, wherever you are
I can hear you, you're a shining star
Singing loud, and singing clear
How beautiful they sound, my dear
My, how they balance
The angels, and their talents
On the branches, of the trees
Calling on, their family, and friends
Chirping happily
Thank goodness, there's no end
To the angels, we call birds
Sometimes seen, but always heard
The angels, of the sky
Are the birds, flying by

Started 15th March 2024
Finished 16th March 2024

I'm glad I came out

I'm glad I came out, when I did
I wouldn't have seen, the bee
The tiny bird, upon the branch
Nor the squirrel, climbing the tree
And to look, down at me

The bright, spring sun
Shining through, my eyelids
With my eyes, lightly closed
To feel the breeze, making a bid
For the spring freshness, up so close

The spring has sprung
How glorious it is
I not only, saw spring today
Felt I did, smiling my way
I'm glad I came out, when I did, today

15th March 2024

Spring is in the air

Spring is in the air
With every sight
And every sound
Spring is in the air
With very flower
And trees, that surround
Spring is in the air
With every bird, that sings
And bees, that come, humming
Spring is in the air
With baby animals, that are born
As we are, getting up
At the crack, of dawn
Spring is in the air
I can see, and I can feel
The fresh, waking beauty
Of nature, incredible and real

16th March 2024

I saw spring today

You can definitely tell
When it is spring
Seeing the bees
And the birds flying
The daffodils, are out
And fully in bloom
Grass is being cut
The sky is blue
With a few clouds
Passing by
And the sun
Shining bright
I saw spring today
What an amazing sight

15th March 2024

Excuse me Nature

Excuse me nature, pardon me
May I have the pleasure
Of your, company
May I relax, with thee
In thy love, and in thy grace
Within the surroundings
Of this, my perfect place
Seeking the comfort, in your arms
With all the pleasures, of your charms

Excuse me nature, pardon me
May I comment on your beauty
I heard your call
For me, to come out, to thee
While I smile, and have a ball
I know, it's an honour
A pleasure, to see all
The comfort, calm, tranquillity too
Given to me, especially from you
There's no doubt, I'll come again
When I do, it will be then

Started 27th February 2024
Finished 28th February 2024

Such beauty, such love

Nature gives us, respect of plenty
Why can't we do the same, for her
She calms us, cares for us, comforts us
Heals us and, so much more, there

We treat her so cruelly
Like she's nothing at all
We dump our litter, wherever we like
And ruin her beauty, before fall

Nature is young, and beautiful
A blessing, in our lives
It's no wonder, she's fighting back
When we, are destroying, her life

I thank you dear nature, created for us
For shadowing, and surrounding me
To embrace, your beauty and love
I thank thee, gratefully

16th February 2024

The Tranquil Nature

As I did, my journal, this morning
I suddenly came alive
The spark got lit, and I, was alight
I jumped out of bed
And got myself dressed
Then took, a short walk
Around, the corner, to the field
Seeing a lovely lady
I said hi, and stopped to chat
After a while, we went on our way
Then I went, and sat
On a big rock
Surrounded by the trees
I close my eyes
And did some breathing
Listening to the birds
With their, angelic singing
The beautiful breeze
Rustling, through the trees
Heaven sent, amazing, and pure
Incredible peace,
A blessing, that does lure
After a while, I head back home
Fully refreshed, tranquil, and calm
Graced with such beauty
And grateful too
Blessed be the smiles
After the storm, comes shining through

Started 2nd February 2024
Finished 4th February 2024

Thank you, for visiting me

The birds, and the bees
And the rustling of the breeze
Through the trees
Tis nature, that brings
To you, glory, my dear
Saying hello, and how do you do?
I am here, so are you
Welcome to my home
Make yourself comfortable
I'll keep you, safe and warm
Relax my dear, smile and cheer
As I pick you up, with comfort
Love, and a hug
Kissing you, with the tranquil bug
How refreshed, do you feel now?
Recharged, renewed, replenished too
Thank you, for visiting me
And seeing me through
For loving me, like I love you
Thank you, for visiting me
And not, treating me cruel

Started 2nd February 2024
Finished 4th February 2024

The Splendour of Nature

Oh, what beauty, and splendour
The verry blessings
Of our nature
The power, of this beautiful gift
It's strength to boost
And give us, a lift
Went for a walk
At the crack of dawn
To see the sunrise
On the horizon
Feeling the crisp, white frost
Right under, my feet
Hearing it crunch
It sounds, so sweet
listening, to the birds, that sing
While on a rock, I sit on my bum
Breathing in, the fresh, cold air
And feeling my bum, going numb
But worth it, it is, to be fair
To embrace lovingly
The nature we're in
And all its glory
It shows us within
Performing, in its, calm and tranquil way
To inspire your body, and your mind
Leaving you, full of the glow
And at peace, for the rest of the day
That is, the splendour, of nature
Very young, yet very mature

19th January 2024

How Beautiful the Snow

How beautiful, is the snow, outside
It sings like angels, so pure
As it floats softly, by my side
Another kiss, from loved ones for sure

How beautiful, is the snow
The crisp white blanket
Like a cuddle, to comfort us so
With a hot chocolate, and a banquet

How beautiful, is the snow
It fills us with joy
The smiles, from all, with a glow
Surrounding us, calling us, to enjoy

10th December 2023

I love

I love the smell of nature
It fills my heart with joy
I Love to hear the birds sing
A smile, I shall employ
I Love to see the waves in the ocean
Big or small, splashing more
I love to touch the snow on the ground
Crisp and white, like before
I Love to taste the fruits of spring
Sweet and sour ooooooo
I love nature,
And I Love you

Started 13th January 2025
Finished 16th January 2025

The Rainbow of Love and Hope

The Rainbow of love
The Rainbow of hope
The Rainbow showing its colours
That we may cope

The Rainbow of faith
The Rainbow of beauty
The Rainbow spreading joy
The smiles, we see

The Rainbow of positivity
The Rainbow of truth
The Rainbow of calm and peace
Even in her youth

The Rainbow of pureness
The Rainbow at home
The Rainbow in the sky
For better days to come

13th December 2024

Autumn Leaves

Autumn leaves falling
As spring green
As a football field

Autumn leaves falling
As bright yellow
As pretty flowers

Autumn leaves falling
As crunchy
As a chocolate biscuit

Written by Thomas Barnes
(my son Aged 5yrs) year 2000

Harmony

Harmony, is the peace, that is near
Harmony, is love, holding loved ones dear
Harmony, is the river flowing
Harmony, is the nature growing
Harmony, the free birds flying
Harmony, the melody, beautifully sung
Harmony, the music, sentimentally done
Harmony, a female name
Harmony, will remain

9th June 2023

Bumble Bees

Bumble bees
Are striped black and yellow
They are friendly
Fuzzy and mellow
Bumble bees, they fly around
To find the nests
They built on the ground
Pollinating, from the flowers wild
A magnet for the bees
To come inside, for the pollen mild
Although, they carry, very little
They're rewarded, favourably
For their efforts, very simple
Bees are amazing
Gentle, kind and pure
Gliding and flying through the air
Incredible, that's for sure
Flying only, through the day
Sleeping, through the night
Bumble bees and honeybees
Such an incredible sight

13th/14th September 2023

Good Night

Good night sky
Good night stars
Good night nature, that goes far
Good night moon
Good night sun
Go and get, yourself some fun
Good night children, babies too
Good night parents
Coming, to check on you
Good night flowers,
Good night grass
Hope you all, have a blast
Good night birds
Good night bees
And all that settle, in the trees
I am grateful, you're here with me
Here with us all
Around the world, blessed be

23rd August 2023

Nature is

Nature is humble
Nature is young
Nature is vibrant
Nature is strong

Nature is calm
Nature is tranquil
Nature is a smile
Nature is still

Nature is peaceful
Nature is a miracle
Nature is joy
Nature is colourful

Nature is hope
Nature is living
Nature is love
Nature is giving

21st April 2024

In my quiet spot

In my quiet spot
I am sat, on a huge rock
Looking round to see
I am surrounded
By a few beautiful trees
Listening, to the birds
And watching the bees
While upon the Field
Where the daffodils grow
And on the roads
The cars and buses, do go
I close my eyes
To drown out, the Traffic
With my smile, big and Bright
And the peace, that's magic
Just like, the Sunrise
I love It
Treasuring, every moment
In my quiet spot, loving and calm
Embracing, the peace
And the stillness
Where I come, to no harm
And the tranquil Glory
In this natures, beautiful story
The precious time, on my own
It is such a pleasure to be
In my quiet spot, Alone
An honour, to be
In natures company
So grateful, am I
To be at one, with thee
And to feel free
In my quiet spot
Beautiful and warm
And so delicate, to me

3rd April 2024

The tree winking

In my quiet place
Circled, by a few trees
I notice, as I look around
There is, one tree
And it stares, right at me
With one eye, he winks
And a slight smile
Giving me hope
life will get better, in a while
I look back at him
With the breeze, upon my face
A smile, I do be giving back
Humbly, and with grace
Feeling refreshed
With nature, nurturing me
I see the tree winking
And I thank thee

Started 11th April 2024
Finished 12th April 2024

When Robins appear

When a robin is here
A loved one is near
When robins appear
They bring with them, a message
From our loved ones dear
Robins are the messengers
From heaven above
They bring the messages
To you, with love
Today a robin, came to me
Perched on a branch, four feet away
It looked at me, for a minute, or two
Then a whisper, I did hear
Before the robin, flew
You are ok
Everything, is going to be fine
Was the message, from on high
With the messenger, so beautiful and true
One that flies high
In the sky so blue

Started 5th May 2024
Finished 7th May 2024

How the sea meets the sky

I love, how the sea meets the sky
The sea so low, the sky so high
At such a distance
Beautifully combined
Joined together
As the horizon binds
A cloud shaped, like a smile
Another shaped, like a dolphin
The sun is shining bright
And I hear nature calling
Picking up the rubbish
Dumped by passers by
To help the wildlife
Continue to live, and to fly
I love, how the sea, meets the sky
Let's take care of nature
And love her throughout her life

20th May 2024

Chapter six
Depression & Anxiety
Our Trials & tribulations

The Strength you need

The strength you need
For this challenge
Is not in your arms, or legs
It is in your heart

The strength you need
To keep going
Is the feeling in your soul
That will never part

The strength you need
When you look deep within
Is the fire, like the hero
Ready to be thrown, like a dart

The strength you need
Will come to you
When you look deep, within your soul
And your heart too

Because the strength you need
Is not in your arms, or your legs
It remains with you forever
It is in your heart

20th May 2024

Never Forget how Strong you are

Stronger than you, think you are
Self-confident, sensitive, a great start
Tougher, than you credit, yourself for
Thoughtful, talented, and so much more
Ready to go, that extra mile
Relaxed and robust, that's your style
Onwards and upwards, right to the top
Optimistic and original, don't you stop
Never stop, your heart giving
Nice and noble, is never failing
Giving and sharing, of your smile
Gracious, genuine, grateful and gentle

Never forget, how strong you are
Remember the trials, that brought you, so far
You can be, who you wish, to be
Just, hold your head up high, and believe

19th January 2024

You are, You can

You are beautiful
You are amazing
You are joyful
You are blazing

You can laugh
You can smile
You can, be yourself
You can go out, in your style

You are safe
You are sound
You are a gift
You are allowed

You can get through
You can be strong
You can be firm
You can be, where you belong

You are unique
You are special
You are loved
You are grateful

To be blessed
To be seen
To be heard
Where have you been

21st November 2023

I know I have the strength

I know I have the strength
To carry out, my duty
I just need to find it
So that it, can help me
It didn't knock, my door today
I fear it may
Have gone a stray
Or maybe, lost its way
I wonder if strength
Will come tomorrow
If I call him loud and clear
I need you strength
Please come to me, my dear
I need you now, more than ever
To help me through, my day
And help me, to endeavour
To get me on my way
I know I have the strength
Need to find it, without delay

18th March 2024

My Mind, An Empty Room

Physically, I know I am here
But mentally, I'm frightened and lost
I don't know, what to do, or where to steer
With my mind, it's stuck in the frost
Feeling separated, from my mind
Spiralling out of control
The memories, that I once had
Are drowning, in the ocean, so deep below
Further away, my memories seem
I can't catch them, to hold them close
Wanting to wake, from this terrible dream
But I'm afraid, I will lose
My head is becoming empty
Of the memories, I hold dear
I'm drowning with despair
With crippling anxiety, and of fear
I wish, I wish, I wish, I knew
Where my memories, are disappearing too
Like a shell my mind is fragile
I would love to go, that extra mile
So confused, as to where, I sit or stand
Getting irritated as I don't know who I am
Do I know you? Who you are
I am sorry, you come so far
I forget, what day, or what month it is
I stare into space, then laugh to bits
I forget, how to write, and how to spell
I'm getting agitated, can anyone tell
I wake up happy, and upbeat too
At the snap of fingers
I'm very anxious, and scared right through
Please, please, don't ask me to remember
I'm really frightened, my mind, it's not here
I know not, what I do
What I say, or put you through

Please accept, my apologies, to you
From the bottom, of my heart, please do
I am grateful, to have, known you all
Remember me happy, bonkers, and full of soul
Remember the good times, when laughter was here
But not the bad times, do you here

Started 6th January 2024
Finished 9th January 2024

I don't know

I don't know,
Just what, I'm gonna do
I don't know
Where, I'm going to
I don't know
What to eat today
I don't know
What to wear, upon this day
My mind, is so blank
Cause a black hole, swallowed it up
My eyes are so heavy
As I'm tired, but I won't give up
I don't know,
On how, it will be
But I do know
I'm going to bring, positivity

Started 8th March 2024
Finished 10th March 2024

A Dark Knight

He has a name
But what could it be
He ties you down
And holds you tightly
There is no mercy, with this dark knight
He pokes and prods, out of spite
He does not discriminate, take a look
This is your life in his book
Determined to push you over the edge
His joys and laughter, now has led
Into the deepest, darkest night
Where there shines, little or no light
He pursues, to push, you down
This he takes, your only crown
Now, he sees, you are low
He provokes, to make you blow
The suffocation, you are feeling
You cry out, for that healing
What is your name? I ask again
Depression is my name, this is my game
You begin, to smile and grin
As you tell, the dark knight, to hold on tight
He rides away, right out of sight

3rd March 2021

I Ventured Out

I ventured out, on my own today
With no one, by my side
Not even, Snowdrop the dog
For me to hide behind
I, get to the end, of the path
That anxious feeling
Started right back
I try to talk, myself down
To help, comfort and calm
Unsuccessful, in creating peace
The anxiety, works up a storm
My mouth goes dry, I go numb
Hands are sweaty
What a pain in the bum
I head back home
Through the door,
Quickly, I Rome
I sit right down, take a deep breath
And think for a while
Why can't this end
I'd love, to live freely
From depression and anxiety
To give a smile
As I ventured out, for a while

27th April 2023

Feeling Scared

Upon waking, this morning
Feeling scared, I was
I know not of what
Nor, know not of why
But scared, I was feeling
Tearful I became
With this uncertain feeling
Hoping it's not here, to stay
But must, must go away
These positive, happy emotions
Have gone astray
Maybe, they lost their way
Somewhere, during the night
I'd like to seek, them out
And guide them right back
But these negative, sad emotions
Are sticking, like glue
Making me feel, quite blue
Please come, back to me
Positive and happy
We shall go, have fun, and play
Disposing of negative, and sad today

29th August 2023

Today

Today was a good day
Though, it was not perfect
I was here, to see it through

Today wasn't a great day
Yet, it wasn't bad
All my limbs, are intact

Today is cloudy, and is wet
Although, I may not, see the sun
I know the sun, will shine again

Today, I am feeling happy
I may not, have much
But I have all I need, I can smile

Today, I'm not full of health
However, I have a body, that has my back
And a soul to help me grow

Today, I am not, full of knowledge
With, my mind, with my heart
The wisdom, I have, will help endure

Today, the stars will twinkle tonight
I may not, be able to reach them
But I see them, and I hear them
They are saying, I am here, twinkling bright

Today I am not perfect
In a world perfectly created, just for us
Happy am I, with that
And very grateful too

24th September 2023

Believe and go far

You are unique
You are special
You are loved
Never lose hope
And don't, you give up
Look straight ahead, your dreams are right there
Chase them, catch them
Grab them while you dare
Hold on to them tight
And don't, let them bite
Instead, love your dreams
Cherish, your dreams
In this, you'll be alright
Make your dreams, feel secure
Then, when you believe
That you can do
Your dreams will lure you
And pull you, Deep in, very pure
And help you, to endure

30th September 2023

Hip, Hip, Yay

Hip, hip, yay
I managed, to do, the housework, today
Anxiety is tiring, wearing thin
I am able, to finally, grin
Hip, hip, yay
No panic attacks, today
Feeling chuffed, proud of myself
Four months ago, I was overwhelmed
Couldn't cook, couldn't clean
Because of anxiety, cutting deep
Panic attacks, cut to the bone
Have me feeling, all alone
But the support, that I have
Helps to relax, smile and to laugh
To this end, I feel at a calm
Feel safe, away from harm
I had a laugh, today
Hip, hip, yay
The dark knight, is fading away

31st January 2023

Life can be Hard

Life can be hard
When, you know not, where to go
You're stuck in a rut, feeling low
Life can be hard
When, you know not, what to do
You can't find anyone, to turn and talk to,
You're in a slum, want to get out
Feeling alone, scared, and full of doubt
Then someone, comes along
And answers your prayers
They sit right down
Listens deep, within there
Beginning to feel, you're at peace
With talking to someone
Your doubts, start to cease
More relaxed, and happy, you become
Smiling more, as you, feel at home

Started 17th October2023
Finished 25th October 2023

When is this Trial going to end

When is this trial going to end
This anxiety, I wish would bend
It's taken hold
It's taken grip
Holding me back
Is there no dip
Don't want to stay in
But can't go out
Anxiety it's so debilitating, I could shout
Taking out of me, all the energy I own
Crippling me, to the bone
I feel so tired
I feel so drained
Cause of anxiety, is unknown and untamed
This anxiety, is unwelcome
Though it lingers, in your home
To complete its job,
Of bringing, you down
Laughing and crushing you, at every step
Til you sink and drown
Giving you, the harshest of blows
Just to see, your all-time low
When is this going to end
I wish, I wish
That this would bend

16th December 2022

These are the words

I uttered some words, yesterday
They had a huge impact
I must say
A panic attack, it did start
Then I uttered those words
It did settle, and depart

Hello anxiety, how do you do
I know, you are here sweetheart
I can feel you
Just letting you know, that I am safe
And I am not, under threat
You can, settle down now
Thank you, for protecting me, my pet

These are the words
That I did speak
These are the words
That did help me
These are the words
That stopped, in its tracks
A full blown, panic attack

Started 30th March 2024
Finished 1st April 2024

I've come so far

I've come so far
Since October twenty-two
I've come so far
From that year, I was so blue
I was a train wreck
Completely derailed
Tried to do something
But I couldn't, I failed
Jumped so high
I could have, sat on the moon
I stepped, in the garden
But it was too soon
Anxiety, overtook me
I could not control
 Overtime, my anxiety
Took its toll
I did not know, what to do
So drained, and tired, was I
Wondering when, the next attack
Would loom, and pass by
Almost, two years on, I am learning
How to keep positive
And my candlelight burning
Working with, not fighting against
The anxiety
That could not rest
I have come, so very far
Not enemies are we

But friends together, strong in bond
What a star

Started 10th April 2024
Finished 13th April 2024

He's struck again

Here we go again
That dark knight
Has struck again
He wants his revenge
Cause I sent him packing
He picked his day, and he's laughing
Alas, I feel lost and confused
Insecure and vulnerable
I let my guard down
And did smile, that much is true
The dark knight certainly knew
That I was feeling so, so, blue
He did dare
To catch me unaware
He struck, with his best might
Now it's my turn, to stand and fight

13th August 2024

Chapter seven

Life

You only live once, have fun

Lives matter, life matters

Lives matter
The young, and the old
Man and woman
The poor and the rich
Black and white
All cultures, side by side

Life matters
You and me
The birds and the bees
All the mammals
And the fish of the seas
The flowers and the trees
And the plants
Blowing in the breeze

Lives matter, life matters
Flying, walking, or running
Let them be
Life is precious
No matter, how big, or small
Lives matter, life matters
Let them grow, and encourage
Them to stand tall

1st May 2024

Share the Smile

Let's have a game
A game of, share the smile
Smiles go, a long, long way
Even plenty, a mile
You can catch them, like a bug
Contagious, that they be
You can't, sweep them, under the rug
As they'll jump out, on you and me
Smiles can spread joy, happiness too
Please come, and join, the fun
With me, please do
Let's have a game
Of share, the smile
Uplift others, and light up, the world too

Started 27th February 2024
Finished 28th February 2024

You only get one life

You only get one life
Live it, and give it a blast
For each new day, upon which, you wake
Live it, like it's your last
Being at one with nature, I once did
Had a shower, in the thunderstorm
Now that day, I truly lived
I felt so free, happy too
Never, was I connected
To nature, as I was that day, right through
I could breathe, and I could smile
As I gained, that connection
To the outside world, for a while
You only, get one chance, at life
Live it true
Live it, like your last

27th February 2024

What is

What is progress, without the setbacks
The positive, without the negative
And the strength, without weakness
Or a friend, without a relative

What is happiness, without sadness
Life, without death
What is laughter, without crying
As we look straight ahead

What is meekness, without arrogance
To go forward, or to go back
What is history, without future
And the fullness, that we lack

In this, a negative world
There is positive, that shines through
To help us, see the light
When the dark creeps in, to make us blue

8th June June 2023

Busy, Busy, Busy

Busy mind, busy days
Busy world, busy ways
Where does it stop
Or go astray
When do, we settle down
And think of our health, today
We're so busy, rushing around
We don't stop, to think
And here the sounds
Of what we do
To the peace, that surrounds
We're so busy
Busy, busy, busy
No time, to hang about
Can't stand still
To eat, to chat, or to help someone out
With our health, in such decline
Our mental health too
Isn't it, about time
To slow down, take a break
And think about you

9th April 2024

Green, White, and Orange

Green are the leaves
The Emerald Isle glow
White is-the snow
The angels that do flow
Orange is the sunset
In the sky at night
Green is the scenery
What a beautiful sight
White are the clouds, passing by
In different shapes and sizes, in the sky
Orange is the fruit and veg, we eat
Sweet potato, oranges, carrots, what a treat
Green, white, orange
The Irish flag colours
Green, white, orange
Unity between, sisters and brothers

2nd March 2024

Never feel, like you're a burden

Never feel, like you're a burden
We're all here, to help
Never feel, you're on your own
When you need us, just yelp

Never feel, like you're a burden
Your health, is important too
An individual, in your own right
A human being, right through

Never feel, like you're a burden
Your feelings, are just as valid, for sure
With a smile, that will brighten the day
And a heart, that's kind and pure

Never feel, like you're a burden
You are full of grace
With people around, to help you though
Blessed be, you're in, the right place

Started 2nd February 2024
Finished 4th February 2024

Sisters in Arms

Sisters in arms
With, all their charms
Collaborating together
As you, will see
From the creations
They, once have made
Joining them together
Just, to create
One solid project
In the name
Of these, two sisters
Both, in arms
And, with their charms
Coming together
One, two, and three

Started 19th February2024
Finished 20th February 2024

For every book

For every book, I have read
Can go over there, in a bag instead
Ready to give, another chance
For someone else, to have a glance

For every book, I have read
I have enjoyed, just before bed
Reading a chapter, or two, at a time
To help relax, and ease the mind

For every book, I will read
I will continue, as started, indeed
The entertainment, that I find
In reading a book, getting a peaceful mind

I have a few books
I shall keep
But the rest, will go
For others, to dive deep

13th March 2024

Times

In the good times, and the bad
Embrace them both, you'll feel glad
To be embracing, the bad times
You will gain, courage and strength
For the good times, that come around
Take care, and look after them, they won't bend
Value the happy times
In this, they shall, give you joy
Comfort the sad times
With you, they will employ
Laughing with the positive times
And pleasure, you will get
Feeling sorry, for the negative times
Shower them with cuddles, you will be blessed
Treasure the highs
Guide the lows
Look in my eyes
And see the love, that grows

Started 1st January 2024
Finished 3rd January 2024

The injustice of it all

Oh, the injustice, of it all
The bad guys, having a grand ball
Picking and manipulating
Mocking and gaslighting too
They know how to act
To make, and see you, feeling blue
Controlling, and making you, a complete tool
For their sneaky, and bullying ways
To get what they want
Then play the victim, telling their lies
To put you down, make you a fool
So, they can smile, under their disguise
The good guys, on the other hand
Endure with pain, in a saddened land
Getting trashed, made to feel small
Feeling worthless
A nobody at all
From the culprits, who just, won't refrain
Loving their cruel, and heartless game
Not giving a care, of how they make, others feel
Taking happiness, from the innocent
The kind and the loving, not a good deal
Bad guys, are winning, and gaining all
Making the good guys
Loose and fall
Oh, the injustice, of it all

Started 12th March 2024
Finished 23rd March 2024

Sometimes, things don't happen

Sometimes, things don't happen
The way, you want them to
So, you just, have to be
Strong enough, to carry through

You imagine, how you would like
To see, your life, in reality
But the life, you are living
Is far from, the dream, you see

In your dream, and in, your reality
Are so very different
Be it positive, or be it negative
This would be the difference

Sometimes, things don't happen
The way, you'd like them to
So put on a smile, in any case
Be strong, and carry it through

23rd March 2024

Invisible but real

The wind may be invisible
To the eye
But you sure can feel it
When it passes by
On your skin, through your clothes
How the wind flies
And, right up close

Heavenly father
You also, cannot see
But I can feel
When he touches me
He touches, my heart
Loving and warm
The whispers, of guidance
Gently, through the storm

They may not, be seen
But know, they are real
From, the heavens, way above the sky
To the air, we breathe from on high

12th March 2024

The limits we put on ourselves

The only limits, that we have
Are the ones
We put on ourselves
If you want to, live freely
Just like a bird
Learn to leave them, on the shelf
Push yourself forward, to the start
Freely, you can live
With an open heart
As I did once
I left them, up there
My limits on the shelf
Became I, free as the air
I was tranquil, calm and free
As my limits weren't there
To burden me
We can do, what, we put our minds to
Just lose the limits
And have a laugh
Embrace your life
And what, you have
Because, the only limits, that we have
Are the ones, we put on ourselves

Started 25th February2024
Finished 27th February 2024

What life is about

Experiences, are what life is about
They are what life is made of
Dreams come alive, inside and out
They, fly freely, just like a dove

Experiences teach us
And guide us, to learn
Encouraging us, to live
Taking risks, at another turn

If you don't take risks, you're not living
Experiences, can be fun
When you embrace, with full heart and soul
The positivity, that lies, is not dull

Never regret, the experiences, you had
And never, have a doubt
Experiences have, a big part, in your life
Because this, is what life, is about

17th February 2024

Am I here

Am I here, out of love
Or is it, out of duty
I know not, of which it is
But frustrated, I am truly
Yes, I love him, very dearly
But sincerely, is it enough
With my heart, so strong, else where
This is just, so friggin tough
I need to look, deep, within my heart
To get the answers, I need
There's no better, place, and time to start
Then in this moment, indeed
I ask again, in amongst, my stuff
Getting it noted, dually
Am I here, out of love
Or is it, out of duty

Started 14th February2024
Finished 17th February2024

Where do I belong

Where, do I belong
Is it in a poem
Or in a song
Maybe, on a path
Where, my dreams await
For me, to come around

I have a distinctive impression
Of where, my life, may begin
A very strong sense, perhaps
And a feeling, here, deep within

But where is it, do I belong
My purpose, in this life, so true
Am I here, to tag along
Or help others, from feeling blue

Who knows, where we, will end up
Or even, where we belong
But when, we have faith
In all, that we do
Our paths, will be shown, to us
Very clearly, very strong
To this end, tis where, I do belong

16th February 2024

Opportunities and Trials

Opportunities, are in our hands
Opportunities, are what, we can see
When we decide, to take on, our opportunities
In this with faith, they will, set us free

Trials we have, can be uncomfortable
Trials we have, can bring us down
They can make it, difficult to cope
Can even leave us, with a frown

Our opportunities, and our trials
Both have, their own, unique way
To help us, guide us, strengthen us
To move on in life, each day

Though this may seem, to be untrue
But look how far, we have all come through
I am grateful, for my opportunities and trials
And bear not, a frown, but contagious smiles

Opportunities I have, are so, very near
I will not, let slip away
Whilst my trials, I must face
I will embrace, each, and everyday
With a positive mind
And a positive heart
Likewise, a grateful soul
Opportunities and trials, that come my way
My blessings, I will count
As I ride, with the waves, far, far away

9th February 2024

Modern Technology

Well, what can I say
The modern technology, of today
Only the tv, once was technology
Now today, what do we see
Computers and, a mobile phone
With built in cameras
For the pictures we take, as we roam
With social media, and text messaging
Letter writing days, are out
And board games, almost extinct
Surely this isn't what life is about
Shopping online, and banking too
What a lazy world, this has become
With modern technology, being the tool
For the scammer's invasion, so not cool
And mental health, is drowning us all
Bringing us down, so who do we call
There's no-one to talk to, at the end of the line
As artificial intelligence
Is now here, for all time
There is, however, good in modern technology
The upside and the positivity
Such as in, the covid pandemic
We could face time, to chat and see
Our family and friends, while we drink tea
Have fun, and a laugh
To see the new arrivals, into the world
And catch, a photograph
Yes, this modern technology
Has its upsides, yay
And also, its downsides too
Like, in life, nothing is perfect
The modern technology, can, leave us blue
We accept, unlike us, living beings
It can't get drunk, and have, just dealings

And suffer, with hangovers
Wouldn't that be, just so funny
To see, drunk and disorderly
Modern technology

Started 20th December 2023
Finished 23rd December 2023

To connect on such, a deep level

To connect on such, a deep level
With the life, we live, in general
The nature, that brings
So much joy, and so much peace
And, the new people, we meet
I hope, will never cease
And to those, we both love, and adore
The hugs, we share, to show we care
So, they don't have to come for
To know that we're really there

To connect, on such a deep level
With feelings and emotions, of plenty
From the heart, is easy to do
If you open it fully, and courageously
In connecting, in the feelings
And experiences of others
Is a gift, and a blessing, to endure
To gently, but truly, embrace, this incredible gift
In helping others, in the future
Steady does it, as you share a smile
And gratefully giving, others a lift
At least for another mile

28th January 2024

I left my heart in Ireland

I left my heart in Ireland
How hollow and empty, I feel
I left my heart in Ireland
That beautiful country, did steal
My soul is deflated
Tears just want to come
I left my heart in Ireland
Now I want to go back to, where I belong
To the place, where I feel at home

10th June 2024

To Gain the Connection

I've not been going out very often
Maybe once, every two to three weeks
I've lost my connection
With nature outside
I don't feel the call
That once, I did so deep

I haven't been out very often
The connection, I need to regain
By trying to get
To my quiet spot, so peaceful
The gift we have been given
So, to connect with nature again

Nature is inspiring me
Like she has in the past
By going out
To embrace her company
And her love too
I need to get out
To connect, and make it last

I need to connect
And feel of her love so deep
Nature's perfect love
Hugs my heart so free
To hear her calling me
Even in my sleep

4th December 2024

We may have lost you today

We may have lost you today
I do not feel sadness, or blue
But a sense of peace and joy
Of calm, comfort, and happiness too

We may have lost you today
The warmth, and the love
You shared, still shines bright
In our hearts, in every way

We may have lost you today
But heaven gained an angel
Knowing you was a pleasure
The laughter you left, an everlasting treasure

We may have lost you today
But your union, you now have
With your love, your beautiful husband
Forever together, hand in hand

We may have lost you today
But blessed are we
To have known you
Forever in our hearts, you will be

                        To Sue a mum to one a mum to all xxxx

Monday 15th July 2024

Life is a risk

Life is a risk
In this, an uncertain world
To take upon you, this risk
You need to have faith, be on her side
The leap of faith, in all you do
Will tell the story, to you, be true
We all need honesty, in our lives
Not false hopes, empty promises
Or injustice, and their lies
Life is a risk, that much is true
Unstable, as it sounds
We have to make, that move
Life is a risk
Just take a dive
Let fear work for you
Feel free, and alive
Life is a risk
Just take that chance
Leap into tomorrow
And take a glance
For a journey, of a lifetime
In this world we're in
I think it's high time
We let faith, step in

22nd March 2024

Why watch the world go by

Why sit, and watch the world go by
When you, can join in
And see the beauty
That you can enjoy
Just dig deep within
Feel the energy begin
Get up on your feet
Then go find some people
You can meet and greet
Have fun, and have a laugh
Get together, and just act daft
Why sit, and watch the world go by
You could, lose out
If you don't get up
And give it a try

20th May 2024

This is not Goodbye

We may have finally
Laid you to rest
But this is not goodbye
This is the best
The memories, we shared
When, you were here
Are close in our hearts
And filling us, with cheer
The smiles we have
With thoughts of you
The love, you gave
Twas, simple and true
The tears, that fell
With our laughter
Of all the jokes told
And all the banter
Twas a blessing
You were in our lives
Now, where did I put
Those high fives
You, may not, be physically here
But in our hearts,
You are always, very near
This is most certainly
Not a goodbye
As we look to the stars
We see you, looking down
Up there so high

Started 28th September 2023
Finished 4th October 2023

The following two parts of this book are the Introductions to two beautiful ladies.

Part 2 Mrs G.D.Bates

Part 3 Miss Chelsea J Rixon

Both have had their trials and tribulations, and have come through the other side.

Their poems express their thoughts and feelings in their lowest points.

I wanted to introduce them to help share, and shine a light upon their creations, and I feel that their work they have chosen themselves will be a credit to them, and the heart and soul they put into creating their work, hoping you enjoy reading them as they did writing them.

Thank you for reading, enjoy and remember

You are loved
You are enough
You are not on your own

Love to you all xxxx

Part 2

An Introduction to Poetry

written By G.D. Bates

Scrambled thoughts

I lay in bed, staring at a blank page,
My pen at the ready yet my hand is still,
So much running through my mind,
I close my eyes not knowing where to start.

Thoughts scream through my head,
Very soon I'm paralysed by my emotions,
Anger, frustration, grief, fear and pain,
Why them, so young, brought into this world and forgotten,
Why him he tries so hard,
What can I do, there's nothing I can do,
Why is this happening to us?

I can feel the tears stream down my face,
Stop now, please stop, open your eyes.
How do I protect them, please someone hear my voice,
Will we ever have the baby we dream of?
Is he Ok, it must be so hard for him?
Does anyone really understand?
Please stop, I can't breathe,
So much torment, so much pain,
Don't want to think anymore, don't want to feel anymore,
Please just open your eyes...

I look around the room,
It seems a little brighter than before,
My thoughts just a whisper, I look down,
My page no longer blank, my hand no longer still.

By G.D.Bates
08-05-2008

Forget to remember

Hi Nana, how are you?
I'm sorry dear, but who are you?
It's me Nana, your granddaughter,
Of course you are, I'm no fool, would you like a brew?
I went in the garden today and sat in the sun,
Oh how lovely Nana, that sounds like fun,
I went in the garden today and sat in the sun,
Did you really Nana, that's great,
It's nice out there now spring has begun,
I went in the garden today and sat in the sun,
Aww that's nice Nana, I bet that was fun,
I'm sorry dear, but who are you?
It's me Nana, your granddaughter,
Of course you are, I'm no fool, would you like a brew?

To know you are lost somewhere deep in their mind,
Only ever to be found from time to time,
To have someone love you so, so much,
Look at you but not see you,
They forget who you are and look confused,
At all the things you say and do,
Repeated conversations, spoken as if for the first time,
Because you don't want them thinking they're losing their mind.
Frustrated, exhausted and full of despair,
Because one day they wander away,
They get lost, can't find their way home,
A fear of them being all on their own,
You find them and see they're confused and distressed,
You know their mind must be such a mess.
It matters not that they have forgotten your name,
Or that they repeat conversations over and over again,
What matters most is their happiness and safety,
Showing them your love, kindness and empathy,
You take the time to show them you care,
And let them know you'll always be there.

Nana, hey Nana, let's go home,
You shouldn't be out here all alone,
I'm sorry dear, but do I know you?
Yes Nana it's me, your granddaughter,
Of course you are, I'm no fool, would you like to come, have a brew?
Sure Nana, that would be nice,
And Nana, just want you to know... that I love you.

By G.D. Bates 12-03-2024

Moment in time

A moment in time,
A world dressed in white,
Alone on a hill,
Nothing to do but wait.

A pain stricken body
Sits where it fell,
Numbed by the freezing temperatures
Of the early morning air.

Minutes felt like hours
As I shivered from the cold
But relief came,
His voice calling my name.

Fighting his way up the snow covered hill,
Slipping with every other step,
He's soon by my side, checking I'm ok
Before sending me on my way.

As I glance back, he's smiling at me
And that's the moment in time when I knew,
Whenever I needed, in times good or bad,
He'd always be there for his little girl.

By G.D.Bates
22-07-2009

For my dad – David Anderson who has always worked so hard to give his children what they need, the dad every daughter deserves.

You are much loved and I'm very blessed to have you for my dad.

Unconditional

When the tears fall, the rivers come
You know she will cry with you,
When you're feeling down and need a smile
You know she will smile at you,
When your days are dark and you can't see the light
You know she will find it for you,
When your struggle to fight is all but gone
She will put that fight back in you.

Down but never beaten
She rises to any challenge,
Putting others before herself,
Never asking for anything in return.
Always there to hold your hand
When times are looking bad,
The advice she gives is to the point,
Given with the loving heart she has.

When the tears fall, the rivers come
She knows you will cry with her,
When she's feeling down and needs a smile
She knows you will smile at her,
When days are dark and she can't see the light
She knows you will find it for her,
When her struggle to fight is all but gone
You will put that fight back in her.

Not a thing they won't do for one and other,
Love in its truest form,
For a mother and child, the love they share
Is unconditional.

By G.D.Bates
14-03-2010

For my mum – Laura Anderson, the sensitive soul who put her whole heart into motherhood,
You did great and you are so loved, I couldn't have asked for anyone better to call mum.

Borrowed

There's a feeling of emptiness
As we drive down the winding roads,
Raindrops fall on the screen in front,
Although the music plays,
An eerie silence takes hold,
I gaze at the sullen clouds and misted hills
And I wonder, is this it?

A father of a friend I'd made
All those years ago,
A father who I came to love
As if he was my own,
Defending me when times were bad,
With open arms came comfort,
He made me laugh but now I cry,
For gone is my borrowed dad.

His illness came as a shock,
These things, they don't happen to us,
But as time passed, we could not deny
He would soon be taken from us.
So much warning yet still not prepared
As we gathered to say goodbye,
So funny right till the end,
Though sometimes through no fault of his own,
He made us laugh but now we cry,
For gone is our borrowed dad.

My tears fall, my heart aches
And I can barely breath,
As I am left to wonder,
If he knew what he meant to me.
As the sky darkens,
And day turns to night,
Reality dawns, a believers truth,
Our time on Earth is borrowed, eternal life awaits,
And though his time has come to an end,
The imprint he's left in our lives,
Can only be matched by our love,
Sealed forever within his heart.

By G.D.Bates
03-10-2008

Dedicated to the man who treated me like one of his own - My Borrowed dad

JAMES "JIM / JIMMY" GOW 28/08/1953 - 23/09/2008.

Loved and Missed Always!

Shattered reflection

She stands alone in her glass house
Shattering every window and door,
With each stone she throws, it's plain to see,
Her reflection is visible no more.

She points her finger but does not see
Three fingers all pointing right back,
The attention she seeks in the form of woe me,
Leaves others taking the flack.

Her friendship questioned, respect for her gone,
Her loyalty put to the test,
As she tramples on those she claimed to love
In her bid not to be second best.

Can she really not see what she claims them to be
Is the true reflection of her?
Or does she really believe in what she says,
So the truth becomes just a blur.

Insecurities blast through every pane
Reflecting off all who are close,
It's time to stop throwing the stones now,
Or she'll loose those who she loves the most.

By G.D.Bates
06-02-2009

Storms of freedom

A dark cloud, a thousand sorrows,
The pouring rain, a thousand tears,
A split second flash, a thousand openings
To the thunderous roar, a thousand fears.

A glimmer of light, warmth burns through,
The tears begin to slow,
The storms subside, the air freshens
And hope begins to grow.

The sun now bright, there's a joyous glow
And a sense of new beginnings,
A look, a smile and a sigh of relief
To see the lives we hold dear are blooming.

Though the clouds will darken our days
The sun has a secret to share,
For a brighter future where our flowers grow free
The storms come to clear the air.

By G.D.Bates
01-05-2009.

Unwritten reality

When you open it up you can step inside,
It's a place to go when you want to hide,
To get away from all that's real,
To escape to whatever time and place you feel,
You can come and go as you please,
Leaving and returning with relative ease.

You're able to look on as others do their thing,
Engrossed in their lives and all they're doing,
Excitedly following the twists and turns,
The truth of the crimes, you soon will learn,
Star crossed lovers with challenging times,
Houses with ghosts and secrets to find.

You join them on their journeys, but they do not know,
You follow their lives, you go where they go,
You're the unwritten character they cannot see,
But wherever they are, that's where you'll be.

You cannot stay in this world forever,
You know this and it's ok,
But it's a nice little place to escape to,
For having time out and to just get away,
And when you find your day is quiet,
Or at night when you have some free time,
It's nice just to pick up where you left off,
In your world of ghosts, love and crime.
It's perfectly ok to escape sometimes,
But making memories with loved ones is best,
For these are the moments in reality,
That makes you feel truly blessed.

So, when you are ready to come back to you,
Closing the book is all you need to do,
With their lives frozen in time, until you visit once more,
It's time to come back to reality,
Facing all you've avoided before.
It's time to face your own challenges,
It's time to face your own ghosts,
It's time to feel the love through your family,

And to be reminded,
It's your story that matters most.

By G.D.Bates 19-02-2024

Where has the festive spirit gone?

Fleeting memories of Christmases long ago,
Little moments, feeling the magic I once knew,
As a child, surrounded by family,
With decorations, Christmas films and turkey too.
Fun little gifts dear old Santa has left,
Spinning tops, wooden toys and a doll,
Mum and Dad had not much to spare,
But we didn't care, we loved it all.

But as time passes me by,
Can someone tell me please,
Where has the magic of Christmas gone?
Why is the festive spirit hiding from me?

As a woman, that magical feeling returns,
While celebrating the first of many,
With the man I love and family around,
The festive spirit spreads its joy in its plenty,
As a mum, passing down to my children,
Traditions old and new,
That feeling only Christmas brings,
Spreading joy and laughter too.

But as time passes me by,
Can someone tell me please.
Where has the magic of Christmas gone?
Why is the festive spirit leaving me?

As the leaves turn brown and the air grows cold,
We play Christmas songs and films from old,
We try desperately to hold on to that feeling,
But can feel it slipping away,
We tell stories of a night before Christmas,
Ghosts visiting through the night,
A man changed for the better in time for Christmas day.
But as time passes me by,
Can someone tell me please,
Where has the magic of Christmas gone?
Why has the festive spirit left me?

As the years go by, the magic fades,
No longer do people care about Christmas day,
Now a holiday so commercialised,
That festive feeling no longer enough,
Only interested in making money,
Or gifting the expensive stuff.
The world has forgotten, no longer does it care,
About the wonderful festive feeling,
That once was everywhere.

Please Christmas spirit, where have you gone,
With the magic you spread to the world?
Please come back to where you belong.
So many take your magic for granted,
But there are still some who care,
So please, when next Christmas comes round,
Promise that you will be there.

By G.D.Bates
24-01-2024

Part 3

An Introduction To poetry

Written By Chelsea J Rixon

Poppy

Poppy, your name is forever, in our hearts
We all loved you, from the start
In fields of joy, you ran so free
Your presence was forever
God's gift to me
Sadly, you've crossed
The rainbow bridge above
Leaving paw prints, of love
Memories to treasure
And endless love

By Chelsea J Rixon

An Endless Love for you

In my heart, forever you reside
Gone from this world
But eternally tied

A gentle soul, brought joy each day
Now your memories
Forever will stay

Your paw prints fade
But our bond stays true
You are forever, the kindest dog
I ever knew

My dearest Poppy
The truest, most precious soul
With tearful eyes
I will let you go

But I still, and always will
Love you, more than you know

By Chelsea J Rixon

Through the eyes of the wolf

In the moons soft glow, the lone wolf roams
Through forests deep, and mountain homes
Their spirits wild, and hearts untamed
In solitude, their freedom claimed

With eyes that gleam, like stars at night
They howl their songs, pure and bright
In silence deep, their paws do tread
A wanderer, with no path ahead

Through valleys dark, and rivers wide
They run with grace, no need to hide
A creature fierce, yet gentle too
In natures realm, their souls anew

Oh, wolf so bold, in shadows play
Your spirit free, night and day
May you roam, forever more
A wild heart, keen to explore

By Chelsea J Rixon

The Bully within

Anxiety is the bully of our minds
Taunts and torments
A relentless grind
Whispering fears, a never-ending test
Stealing joy and smiles
Leaving the heart distressed
The pestering thoughts, are they true
Or are they memories
Of things I've been through
I don't know whether to shout or cry
But these memories remain,
No matter what I try

By Chelsea J Rixon

In the mind

In shadows of doubt, anxiety grips tight
A prison unseen, a relentless fight
Chains of worry
Bind the soul with fear
But within the darkness
Hope draws near
Through trembling steps, and courage found
Break free from, the walls
That continue, all around

By Chelsea J Rixon

A story told

Etched upon the skin,
Are the stories of pain
Scars of battle worn
Not worn in vain
Each mark is a story told
Beauty is found, with strength
Resilient and bold
Embracing my imperfections
My flaws are art
Scars shining brightly
Like a warrior's heart

By Chelsea J Rixon

Trauma

Trauma's grip, can alter one's core
Leaving marks unseen, forever more
Physical touch, may bring a shiver
A reminder of wounds,
That forever linger
Yet in time, with care and grace
Love and hope
Can fill, the empty space

By Chelsea J Rixon

Survivor

In shadows deep, a silent cry resounds
A survivor's heart in solitude, it drowns
Bound by memories, a prison of my mind
Loneliness echoes, leaving scars behind

By Chelsea J Rixon

Through the eyes of a survivor

In the wreckage of my past, I rise
A survivor's spirit, strong and wise
Through darkness and pain
I found light
In some strength, I take flight

By Chelsea J Rixon

A Safe Sanctuary for me

In the realms of dreams
Where shadows dance
Lies a sanctuary where only
Loved ones can glance

A bed, a refuge
A place of rest
Where worries fade
And the soul is blessed

Within the embrace
All fears subside
A fortress of comfort
Where love resides

No harm can reach
No evil can stay
At the door
Should thoughts and demons stay

In this world, time stands still
The world can fade away

By Chelsea J Rixon

Unlikely Hero

In the quiet of night, their love shines bright
Silent heroes in shadows, out of sight
Through gentle guidance, and unwavering care
Parents stand strong, hearts pure, and rare

Their sacrifice, known to few
In every hug, a secret scream, I love you
With a silent strength, they face each day
Nurturing and protecting, along the way

In whispered tones, and unspoken fears
Their love continuously grows
Through the years
Our silent heroes, we owe you so much
For your protectiveness, touch

By Chelsea J Rixon

Medication is Hope

In pills and potions, hope we seek
To calm the storm
Including ones, we dare not speak
Yet in the mind, the battle rages on
Medications grip, not always strong

Anxiety whispers, like a relentless tide
Depressions weight
Leaves it hard to hide
Inner demons, making chase
Leaving a struggle, for a dry face

Side effects, and empty stares
A silent scream, nobody shares
In the maze, of minds despair
Medication can falter, leaving us bare

But a flicker of light,
Offers hope, on the darkest night

By Chelsea J Rixon

A Gamers Life

In pixels and codes, a new self takes flight
Through screens and controllers
A world so bright
A gamers heart, beats to a digital drum
Transforming, into a hero
Fearsome and glum

With courage and skin, they face every foe
In virtual realms, where dreams can grow
A new personality, forged in games fire
Embracing challenges, reaching
Higher and higher

Their characteristics, moulded by quests untold
In adventures vast, their stories unfold
From shy to bold
Gaming shapes them, where they belong

In pixels and code, a transformation complete
A gamers spirit soars, destiny sweet
With new traits and qualities, to show
Gaming has made them, truly glow

By Chelsea J Rixon

The poems in this book are based on gratitude, what I am grateful for, and the little, simple, basic things in life that we take for granted, ignoring them as being our blessings, including that of our trials and tribulations, that can make us stronger, which of course, I am also guilty of this. As we go about our lives rushing around, we fail to take notice of the things and people in our lives that really matter, we don't take time out to notice, and really notice, the more beautiful things going on, and that surrounds us, we don't take the time out we need and to slow down. The poems in this book are about slowing down, being grateful for what, and who you have in your lives, to slow down reflect and take care of ourselves and be ourselves, something again I am also guilty of, Like many of you in the world I have my downs, yet I also have my ups, both ups and downs I am grateful for, I try to embrace both ups and downs, negative and positive to the best of my abilities.

Life is and, can be hard to get through day to day, but by using the gift of gratitude just for the tiny things in life, you become happier and a magnet to the bigger, brighter blessings in your life.

It's not when we die, it's how we live that's important, we only live once, live each day as if it's your last, have fun, live, laugh & love.

www.ingramcontent.com/pod-product-compliance
Lightning Source LLC
Chambersburg PA
CBHW022105090426
42743CB00008B/720